Food For Thought

{ Cultivating Well-being Through Health }

By: Chiadi Kobi

Table of contents

Chikobi Health's Cultivating Well-Being 4
The Eightfold Path: Applied Wisdom 5
The Eightfold Path: Reflection & Action Steps 7
Lojong Slogans For Daily Life 9
Petitionary Prayer: Beyond Self 11
Weaving Prayer Into Your Daily Tapestry 13
Ecotherapy 14
Cognitive Emotional Pedagogy 15
Metaphorical Learning 17
Exploring Implicit Biases 20
50 Voices, One Journey 22
Practice Your Go-To Phrases 24
Building Your Toolkit Of Phrases 25
Mindful Anchoring: Emotional Regulation 26
The Mindful Anchoring Practice 28
Integrating Anchoring Into Daily Life 30
Managing Chronic Pain With Practice 31
Integrating Wellness Into Pain 32
Posture Practice For Pain 33
Stretching And Movement 35
Mindful Posture Awareness 37
Ergonomics At Home And Work 38
Aromatherapy For Well-Being 39
Reflexology For Holistic Healing 41
Acupressure For Balance 42
Empowering Well-Being Through Food 43
Benefits Of Home Cooking 45
Integrate Harmony In Daily Life 47
Reflective Budgeting 49
Your Health Story 50
Building Community 53
Global Wellness Practices 55
Natural Movement - Global Traditions 56
Ancient Traditions 58
...Wisdom From Across The World 60
Cultural Healing: Embracing Restoration 61
Isha Kriya Meditation 62
Three Cycles Harmonizing Body And Mind 64
Your Journey Forward 66

CHIKOBI HEALTH'S CULTIVATING WELL- BEING

Welcome

In these pages, you will embark on a transformative journey that traverses various cultures and traditions, offering a blend of practical tips, ancient wisdom, and effective techniques to enrich your mental, physical, and spiritual well-being.

Within these pages, you'll find:

- Timeless teachings to enrich your perspective
- Tools to shape your personal narrative
- Nature-based activities to calm the mind
- Complementary health techniques for balance
- A supportive community of fellow seekers

This experience is about more than just treating symptoms. It's about nurturing your whole self - mind, body and spirit.

When we take time to care for our wellbeing, reflect on our stories, and connect with a compassionate community, we can build lives of greater meaning and resilience.

Be open to new insights that may arise as you engage with the material ahead. This is your time to slow down, turn inward, and emerge renewed.

"Food for Thought" is designed to be your companion
in a journey towards a more fulfilling life, where you are encouraged to engage deeply with the content, practice mindfulness, and embrace the joy of cooking as an integral part of your health and well-being journey.

May this be an opportunity to cultivate your growth, and transform your world.

The Eightfold Path: Applied Wisdom

It's believed that ancient teachings can shed light on our contemporary quest for wellness. The Eightfold Path, a core component of Buddhist philosophy, offers us a blueprint for living a life balanced in ethics, awareness, and mental discipline - all crucial for holistic health. Below, we delve into each aspect of the Path, offering a perspective on how they can be integrated into our daily routines to promote physical, mental, and spiritual well-being.

Right Understanding

Mindful Education: Engage in continual learning about health and wellness. Understand how lifestyle choices affect your well-being. Recognize the impact of diet, exercise, stress, and relationships on your health.

Holistic Perspective: Acknowledge that your health is multi-dimensional. Consider how emotional and spiritual health affects physical health and vice versa.

Right Thought

Positive Affirmations: Replace negative self-talk with positive affirmations. Cultivate a growth mindset that recognizes challenges as opportunities for personal development.

Vision of Wellness: Visualize your health goals and what a balanced life looks like for you. Let this vision guide your daily choices.

Right Speech

Constructive Communication: Foster healthy relationships through empathetic and honest communication. Share your health journey with others in ways that inspire and uplift, not judge or belittle.

Self-Dialogue: Be aware of your internal dialogue. Speak to yourself with kindness as you would to a dear friend, especially in times of illness or stress.

Right Action

Healthy Behaviors: Make choices that honor your body and health. Whether it's regular exercise, nutritious eating, or adequate sleep, act in ways that nurture your well-being.

Community Involvement: Volunteer, support, or engage in community events that promote health and wellness. Right action includes social responsibility.

Right Livelihood

Purposeful Work: Align your professional life with your values. If possible, choose a career that contributes positively to the well-being of others and feels meaningful to you.

Balance and Boundaries: Establish boundaries to prevent work-life imbalance that can lead to burnout. Prioritize time for self-care and family.

Right Effort

Persistent Practice: Cultivate healthy habits with consistent effort. Wellness is a journey, not a destination, and requires ongoing commitment.

Adaptable Resilience: Be prepared to adapt your efforts to changing life circumstances, always with the goal of personal and communal well-being in mind.

The Eightfold Path: Reflection & Action Steps

Where could you make changes to align more closely with these principles? Reflect on how even small shifts can create significant positive change in your health and happiness. Choose one aspect of the Eightfold Path to focus on this week. Set practical goals for incorporating its wisdom into your daily life. These practices invite you to weave these age-old principles into the fabric of your modern life.

Put in practice

1. Right Speech

Giving a genuine compliment each day

2. Right Effort

Setting a regular bedtime to ensure you get enough rest

Right Mindfulness

Intentional Presence: Incorporate mindfulness exercises into your routine to enhance presence. Practice mindful eating, walking, or even working to deepen your connection to the present moment.

Awareness in Action: Bring a quality of attention to your daily activities. Notice the sensations of movement during exercise or the flavors in your meal to enrich your experiences.

Right Concentration

Focused Calm: Develop concentration through practices such as meditation or deep breathing exercises to calm the mind and reduce stress.

Single-Tasking: Encourage a focused approach to tasks. Multitasking can lead to stress and inefficiency, whereas single-tasking can lead to higher quality engagement and productivity.

Lojong Slogans for Daily Life

Incorporating Lojong into your daily life can have a transformative effect on your mental landscape. With each step, you cultivate a garden of wisdom, compassion, and mindfulness that can sustain you through the ebbs and flows of life. Let these slogans be your companions, whispering guidance and encouragement as you journey toward holistic well-being.

Lojong is a Tibetan Buddhist practice of using pithy slogans to reshape our habitual thought patterns and cultivate wisdom and compassion.

Let's reflect on a few key Lojong slogans:

LOJONG WISDOM

"Regard all dharmas as dreams"

Consider how each experience and phenomenon arises temporarily like a dream. Let go of attachment and aversion. Be present.

"Examine the nature of unborn awareness"
Look beyond the superficial identity to recognize the unchanging pure awareness within all.

Realize unity.

"Rest in the nature of alaya, the essence"
Return to a natural, open, relaxed state beyond conceptual thought. Let the mind rest in its basic essence.

"In post-meditation, be a child of illusion"
After meditation, maintain the mindset of seeing phenomena as illusions. Refrain from clinging or pushing away.

Integrating these slogans into daily life can gradually reshape our mental patterns. Notice how they allow thoughts and emotions to simply pass through awareness without grasping. This reduces unconscious reactions, bringing wisdom, equanimity and compassion.

Lojong's aphorisms slogans provide accessible yet profound guidance. Their practice develops presence, non-judgment and insight into the nature of self and reality. Our thoughts need not define us when we regard them as passing dreams.

Put in practice

Nature Connection

Illusion Play

Reflective Journaling

Mindful Morning

Routine

Empathy Practice

Compassionate

Communication Exercise

Mindful Eating

Active Kindness

Petitionary Prayer: Beyond Self

Petitionary Prayer, a deeply personal and spiritual practice, extends beyond mere words spoken or thought. It's a heart-to-heart dialogue with a higher power, a sacred conversation where we express our deepest desires, concerns, and gratitude.

A Bridge Between Breath and Belief

Amidst the bustling rhythms of life, the human spirit yearns for connection, for a sense of belonging. This practice offers a conduit for channeling our hopes and fears beyond the limitations of the ego.

And there's profound beauty in the way petitionary prayer intertwines with the very essence of life: our breath. Each inhale draws us inwards, connecting us to a force greater than ourselves, while each exhale carries our petitions outward, releasing them into the universe.

In the context of the 'breathe in, breathe out' philosophy, meditation represents the inward breath - a moment of introspection, of internal peace and self-awareness. In contrast, petitionary prayer is the outward breath - an active expression.

BEYOND WORDS

Combine with Movement

Embrace Community

Reflective Journaling

Mindful Walks

Introspect the Day

Anxiety Release

Science Supports the Power of Prayer

Research reveals a compelling connection between prayer and well-being. Studies conducted by institutions like Duke University and Stanford University have shown that regular prayer leads to reduced stress and anxiety, enhanced feelings of happiness, and even greater longevity.

These findings suggest that the act of connecting with a divine force, of relinquishing our burdens and trusting in something greater, fosters a sense of peace and calm that ripples through our physical and mental landscapes.

Prayer is an integral spiritual practice that has potential to enhance overall well-being.

Weaving Prayer into Your Daily Tapestry

Ultimately, the true power of petitionary prayer lies not in the words or rituals, but in the genuine connection you cultivate with a greater force. By opening your heart, weaving prayer into your breath, and trusting in the unseen, you invite peace, purpose, and well-being into your daily life.

Find Your Sanctuary
Create a dedicated space, be it a quiet corner in your home or the serene embrace of nature, where you can connect with your inner peace and focus on prayer.

Embrace Simplicity
Prayer doesn't require elaborate rituals or eloquent pronunciations. All you need is an open heart and genuine words that resonate with your emotions and desires.

Start With An Invocation
Connect with your chosen higher power, using a familiar prayer or simply expressing your intention to connect with something greater.

Focus Your Intention
Clearly define your needs and desires. This could be a personal concern, a wish for someone you love, or an expression of gratitude for blessings received.

Release and Trust
Once you've voiced your petition, release it with trust. Open your heart to potential answers and guidance, which may come in subtle ways beyond words.

End With Gratitude
Expressing thankfulness reinforces the positive energy of your prayer and fosters an attitude of acceptance.

With these practices, you are not only stepping into a space of personal healing but also contributing to the collective wellness of the world. Let this guide you in nurturing this vital relationship with the natural world, fostering resilience, and inspiring a balance within.

Put in practice

Step 1: Find a natural setting like a park, garden or forest trail. Tune into your senses as you take in the environment.

Step 2: Walk slowly and mindfully for 10-15 minutes. Notice sights, sounds, smells and sensations without judgment.

Step 3: Pause to take some deep breaths. Observe how the air feels entering your nose and lungs.

Step 4: Sit quietly for a few minutes, feeling connected to the earth. Hand on heart. Feel your inner resources.

Step 5: Journal or share reflections afterwards. Did you gain any insights from this time in nature?

Ecotherapy

Deepening Our Connection with Nature. Welcome to the realm of ecotherapy, where the healing embrace of the natural world meets the inner sanctum of the human spirit. It is understood that our connection to Earth is not just a luxury, but a vital component of holistic wellness. This section invites you to deepen that connection through immersive activities and reflective practices that align body, mind, and spirit with the rhythmic pulse of nature.

14

Cognitive Emotional Pedagogy

Humans are wired to learn best through actively doing rather than just passively studying concepts. We also emotionally connect more with narratives rather than just dry facts. Leveraging these insights; this emerging training method seeks to blend critical content with evocative delivery and relatable applications for daily practice.

Nurturing Minds, Health, and Souls: Exploring Experiantial Learning

Education often finds itself confined to sterile textbooks and formulaic tests. But true learning transcends intellectual execises; it encompasses a vibrant dance between cognition and emition, shaping not just our minds but our hearts and souls as well. We delve into the relm of Cognitive Emotional Pedagogy (CEP), an innovative approach that recognizes the power of emotions in fostering meaningful learning and well-being.

Control-Value Theory: Where Emotions Takes the Lead

At the core of CEP lies the understanding that emotions play a crutial role in influencing our thoughts, behaviors, and ultimately, our learning experiences. Control-Value theory, formulated by psychologist Albert Ellis, suggests that our emotional responses are determined by two key dimensions: valence (positive or negative) and activation (high or low).

According to the theory, the most impactful emotions fall into the high-activation categories, regardless of whether they are positive (excitement, enthusiasm) or negative (anxiety, anger).

Affective Pedagogy: Emotions in the Driver's Seat

This is where affective pedagogy comes into play. This teaching approach actively seeks to engage an individuals' emotions; creating an atmosphere that fosters positive emotional valence and high activation. This isn't about manipulating emotions; instead it's about creating a climate conducive to genuine engagement, exploration, and discovery.

Kyriacou's Social Pedagogy: A Holistic Framework

The philosopher Christos Kyriacou further expands on this concept through his Social Pedagogy. He proposes a five-dimensional framework that emphasizes the needs of the whole self, rather than just intellectual prowess. These dimensions include:

Care: Building a culture of empathy, warmth, and respect, ensuring everyone feel safe and supported.

Inclusion: Fostering a sense of belonging and valuing the unique contributions of each individual.

Socialization: Cultivating social skills and emotional intelligence, equipping ourselves to navigate relationships effectively.

Educational Support: Providing differentiated instructions and guidance to cater to individual styles and needs.

Social Eduacation: Promoting critical thinking about social issues and personal growth.

Metaphorical Learning

Metaphorical learning is a transformative tool that transcends the literal to offer rich, symbolic avenues for personal growth and healing. It is here that we harness the power of imagery to shape our journey towards wellness. Experts advocate for the use of metaphorical learning as an integral component of self-discovery and empowerment.

Exploring Personal Metaphors

Visualize a mountain to represent your current challenges. Are you at the base, gathering strength for the climb? Halfway up, facing the steep and rocky path? Or near the summit, ready to embrace the expansive view?

Reflect on the image of a river. Consider how it mirrors your life's journey — sometimes flowing smoothly, other times encountering rapids or obstacles that require navigation. What can this river teach you about resilience and adaptation?

Empowering Metaphors for Change

If your life feels like a maze, reimagine it as a labyrinth. Unlike a maze, a labyrinth has a clear path to the center and back out, symbolizing a journey to the heart of oneself and the way forward.

Replace the metaphor of being stuck in quicksand with the image of a potter shaping clay. This signifies that you have the creative power to mold and reshape your life's circumstances.

Interactive Metaphorical Activities

Create a vision board that illustrates your desired future using images, words, and symbols that inspire and motivate you towards your goals.

Engage in a guided visualization where you picture yourself in a serene landscape that reflects peace and healing. What elements are present? A gentle stream, a sturdy oak tree, a vibrant garden?

Daily Metaphorical Reflections

Start or end each day by selecting a metaphor that embodies your current state or intentions. Use it as a focal point for meditation or journaling.

When faced with decisions or obstacles, ask yourself which metaphor best represents your approach. Are you a warrior ready for battle or a diplomat seeking peace?

Reframing with Metaphorical Learning

If you find yourself identifying with the metaphor of a storm cloud, consider what it would mean to be the sky — vast and unchanging, capable of weathering any storm.

Replace the symbol of a closed door with that of an open window, suggesting that although one opportunity may seem lost, another perspective or avenue is available.

Exploring Implicit Biases

Our implicit biases refer to unconscious attitudes or stereotypes that can influence our behaviors and decisions in ways we don't consciously intend. These biases arise from our internalized beliefs, experiences, and societal conditioning. Examining and reflecting on our implicit tendencies is key for growth.

Put in practice

Diverse Exposure

Perspective-Taking

Feedback Seeking

Counter-Stereotyping

Allyship Actions

Check Biases in Decision-Making

Implicit Bias Training

Continuing Education

Consider exploring an online implicit association test (IAT) offered by organizations like Project Implicit. These short activities can uncover hidden biases we may hold around areas like race, gender, age, and more.

Additionally, here are some reflective exercises Recall situations where you felt discomfort. Explore potential implicit biases at play.

Notice when you assign characteristics to someone prematurely. What assumptions come up?

Reflect on how biases affect your relationships and communication style with different groups.

Examine your own identity. What societal biases do you carry regarding your own groups?

Envision you had a different identity. How would it shape your perspective and biases?

While confronting biases can feel uncomfortable, this discomfort signifies an opportunity for increased awareness. Being aware of our biases is the first step in growth. Cultivating compassion starts with compassion towards our own humanness.

50 Voices, One Journey

Insight bubbles up in the most unexpected places. As we connect with fellow travelers crossing life's lanscapes, nourishing truths emerge through stories and perspectives not our own. This calls us to lift our gaze and open our ears. As you contemplate these questions, allow your answers to unfold organically. Consider using them as conversation starters.

Exploring the Depths of Human Connection
In a world often saturated with noise and distraction, true connection can feel like a rare treasure. We yearn for authentic interactions, for glimpses into the hearts and minds of others that transcend the surface chatter of daily life. The web series "50 People, One Question" embarks on a poignant journey, capturing the raw essesnce of human connection through a simple yet powerful premise: asking 50 individuals from diverse backgrounds a single, thought-provoking question.

But this series is more than just a collection of answers. It is a tapestry woven with threads of hope, vulnerability, and shared humanity.

As we listen to the voices of strangers, from bustling city streets to tranquil countryside villages, we are invited to delve into the depths of our own lives, reconnecting with our own purpose, dreams, and aspirations.

Imagine embarking on a virtual journey yourself, meeting these 50 individuals and hearing their responses to questions that resonate with our deepest yearnings.

Questions for Reflection

What is your one purpose in life?

What is your one dream for tomorrow?

Where would you wish to wake up tomorrow?

What do you wish to happen by the end of the day?

If you could be any age, what age would you be?

If you could change one thing about your body, what would it be?

Encouraging Self-Exploration and Acceptance

Each question presented here is a stepping stone on an ever-evolving path of self-discovery. There are no right or wrong answers, only the echos of your own unique experience. As you journey through life's labyrinthine turns, revisit these questions. Allow them to be your companions, guiding you towards deeper understanding, acceptance, and ultimately, the profound beauty of simply being.

Practice Your Go-To Phrases

Communication often becomes a hurried exchange of words, deviod of the mindful awareness that fosters genuine connection and wellbeing. Yet, our language, the very fabric of our interactions, holds immense power to uplift, inspire, and create a positive climate.

The Pitfall of Unintentional Words. Consider the familiar Monday morning office scene. The leader throws out a cheerful, "How's everyone doing?" and receices a chorus of polite, "Good!"s or shrugs. But beneath the surface, a colleague might be grappling with personal struggles, a weekend mishap, or a lingering health concern. This seemingly innocuous question, with its implied expectation of a positive response, can inadvertently exclude those who genuinely need support or simply crave authentic connection.

This, friends, is the biggest, most easily avoided error in emotional intelligence: saying things off-the-cuff without contemplating their potential emotional impact. We may not intend to cause harm, but hastily thrown words can trigger discomfort, isolation, and a sense of being unseen.

Shifting from Auto-Pilot to Intentional Expression. So, how do we navigate this communication minefield and cultivate go-to phrases that foster emotional well-being and connection? Here are some key shifts:

From Platitudes to Empathy. Replace generic phrases with expressions that ackowledge the complexities of human experience. "I hope you had a restful weekend" acknowledges the possibility of challenges while offering well wishes.

From Closed to Open-Ended Questions. Instead of prompting expected answers, ask questions that invite genuine sharing and connection. "What's something you're looking forward to this week?" or "Are there any challenges you'd like to share?" open the door for meaningful conversation.

From Self-Centered to Inclusive. Shift your focus from your own experience to those around you. Instead of "I'm swamped!", consider "What support might you need this week?"

24

Building Your Toolkit of Phrases

Let's delve into the practice of cultivating go-to phrases, intentional expressions that guide our conversations and interactions with emotional intelligence and empathy. Here are some examples of mindful phrases you can integrate into your daily communication.

Go-To Phrases for Daily Practice

Greetings: "Good morning everyone! I'm excited to see what we can accomplish together today." (Instead of the generic "How's everyone doing?")

Offering Support: "If anyone needs anything this week, please don't hesitate to reach out. We're in this together."

Ackowledging Challenges: "I know these can be tough times, so please know we have each other's back."

Expressing Gratitude: "I'm truly grateful for this team and everything we do together." Promoting Connection: "What are some things you've been passionate about lately? I'd love to hear more."

The Ripple Effect of Intentional Communication

Remember, every word we speak creates ripples that reach far beyond the moment of utterance.

Make a conscious effort to practice your go-to phrases, and witness the transformative power of language in your daily life.

Mindful Anchoring: Emotional Regulation

Welcome to "Mindful Anchoring," a transformative practice designed to enhance your emotional well-being and self-awareness. In today's fast-paced world, it's easy to feel overwhelmed by emotions and external pressures.

Life moves fast. Between work, family, and the constant ping of technology, our attention gets pulled in endless directions. Stressful events can trigger unhelpful emotional reactions before we even realize what's happening. Practices that cultivate mindfulness - present-moment, non-judgmental awareness - equip us with tools to stay grounded and intentionally shape our responses.

Mindful anchoring trains us to find focus through external sensory cues that keep us anchored in the here and now. For example, consciously noticing sensations like the feel of your feet on the floor, the sound of birds chirping outside, or the aroma of coffee can quickly reconnect you with the present when the mind wanders.

With regular practice, mindful anchoring builds the mental muscle memory to recognize unhelpful emotional reactions more quickly and prevent them from escalating. It allows us to name emotions, understand their origins, and choose thoughtful actions aligned with our values. Over time, this emotional intelligence ripples through all areas of life. This simple but profound technique also expands awareness beyond our narrow perspective to see our place within the broader community and world. With greater consciousness comes greater compassion.

Are you ready to drop anchor and cultivate emotional balance? Let's explore how to put mindful anchoring into practice.

The Mindful Anchoring Practice

At ChiKobi Health, we understand the power of mindfulness in transforming lives. This step-by-step guide is a pathway to developing a deeper understanding of your inner world and how it interacts with the environment around you. Through this practice, you will learn to navigate your emotions with greater ease, allowing for a more harmonious balance between your inner self and external realities.

Step-by-Step Guide

1. Contextual Awareness

Begin by immersing yourself in the present moment. Acknowledge the details of your environment and the activity you are involved in. Describe your setting and the frequency of this activity in your life. For example, "It's a serene Sunday morning, I am at home indulging in my hobby of painting, a creative escape I cherish weekly."

2. State of Mind and Well-being Assessment

Each session starts with a sincere self-reflection of your current mental and emotional state. Express openly or write down your immediate feelings and the reasons behind them. Strive for specificity to gain clear insights. For instance, "At this moment, I feel a sense of calm mixed with anticipation for the week ahead, balancing my professional responsibilities and personal desires."

3. Micro to Macro Perspective

Broaden your perspective from personal surroundings to a larger context. Reflect upon your role and influence in the broader scope of your community, society, and the universe. For instance, "As an individual, my daily choices and interactions contribute to the collective energy of my community, influencing our shared experiences and societal growth."

4. Future Visualization

Look ahead and visualize your future self. Contemplate different aspects of your life trajectory – personal achievements, career goals, and interpersonal relationships. For instance, "Looking forward, I envision myself in a state of continued growth, achieving professional milestones while nurturing meaningful relationships and personal well-being."

5. Unconscious Manifestation

Encourage these visualizations to subtly influence your subconscious mind. Trust in the power of regular reflection to guide your daily decisions, steering you towards your envisioned future.

Integrating the Practice
Adopting Mindful Anchoring into your daily life signifies your dedication to enhancing your mental and emotional wellness. This guide serves as your companion in this enriching journey, offering a structured approach to cultivating mindfulness and emotional resilience. Embrace this practice as a key component of your path towards holistic health, in line with the principles and mission of ChiKobi Health.

Integrating Anchoring into Daily Life

Implementing Mindful Anchoring into your daily routine is a commitment to your mental and emotional health. By incorporating. Mindful Anchoring into your daily life, you're taking a significant step towards achieving a balanced, fulfilling life.

Tips to Make the Most Out of This Practice

Consistency is Key: Practice Mindful Anchoring three times a day – morning, noon, and night. Consistency helps solidify this habit.

Create a Mindful Space: Find a quiet spot where you can practice without interruptions. This space can be anywhere – your home, office, or even a park.

Journaling: Consider keeping a journal to track your thoughts and progress. Writing can provide insights into your emotional patterns and growth.

Mindful Reminders: Set reminders on your phone or computer to take a few minutes for your practice, ensuring you don't skip it during busy days.

Share Your Experience: If comfortable, share your experiences with friends or family members. Discussing your journey can provide additional insights and support.

MANAGING CHRONIC PAIN WITH PRACTICE

Chronic pain, a pervasive issue affecting a significant portion of the population, extends beyond mere physical discomfort, impacting mental health and overall quality of life.

Chronic Pain Management

Effective management requires a comprehensive approach that encompasses understanding the nature of pain, its triggers, and the holistic methods available for mitigation.

Understanding Chronic Pain

Chronic pain is defined as pain that persists beyond the normal healing time of three months. It can be continuous or intermittent, varying in intensity. Unlike acute pain, which serves as a warning signal of injury, chronic pain often remains long after the initial injury has healed, due to changes within the nervous system.

The Importance of Posture

Posture plays a crucial role in managing chronic pain. Poor posture can exacerbate pain conditions by straining muscles and joints. Conversley, correct posture can alleviate pain, improve mobility, and prevent further injury. These sections will highlight the significance of maintaining a neutral spine position and adopting ergonomic practices in daily activities to support the body's natural alignment.

Strategies for Pain

Managing chronic pain is a dynamic process that involves a combination of physical, psychological, and lifestyle strategies. By understanding the underlying factors contributing to pain and implementing daily practices focused on posture, mindfulness, and overall well-being; individuals can achieve a better quality of life.

Integrating Wellness Into Pain

Adopting a holistic approach to pain management involves integrating physical, emotional, and spiritual wellness practices. This comprehensive strategy recognizes the individual as a whole and seeks to address the root causes of pain, rather than just the symptoms.

Holistic Approaches to Pain Relief

- Physical Wellness. Incorporating regular, gentle exercise tailored to one's condition, such as yoga or swimming, which can improve strenght, flexibility, and endorphine levels, helping to naturally reduce pain sensations.
- Emotional Wellness.Techniques such as journaling, counseling, and support groups or clubs can provide emotional outlets and coping strategies, reducing the stress and anxiety that often accompany chronic pain.
- Spiritual Wellness. Practices like meditation, deep breathing exercises, and mindfulness can enhance one's sense of well-being, offering peace and acceptance in the journey of managing chronic pain.

The Role of Diet and Nutrition in Pain Management

Diet plays a significant role in managing inflammation, which can contribute to chronic pain. Incorporating anti-inflammatory foods into your diet, such as omega-3 fatty acids found in fish, antioxidants in berries, and phytochemicals in leafy greens, can help reduce inflammation and pain levels. Additionally, staying hydrated and limiting processed foods can support overall health and aid in pain management.

Integrating wellness practices into your daily routine can significantly enhance your quality of life by managing chronic pain more effectively. By embracing a holistic approach that includes physical activity, emotional support, spiritual practices, and a balanced diet, you can empower yourself to take control of your pain and lead a more fulfilled life.

Posture Practice for Pain

In our digital age, many of us spend hours sitting at desks, which can contribute to chronic pain if not done correctly. Proper sitting posture is crutial for minimizing stress on the spine and preventing pain.

> **Put in practice**

Incorporating these posture practices into your daily activities can significantly impact your comfort and wellbeing. Remember, making small adjustments to your posture can lead to signifcant improvements in how you feel daily.

Sitting Posture for Health and Wellbeing

Align Your Back. Sit back in your chair with a lumbar support pillow at your lower back to maintain the spine's natural curve. Your buttocks should touch the back of your chair.

Monitor Height and Distance. Position your computer screen at eye level and about an arm's lenght away. This prevents you from straining your neck and eyes.

Feet and Arms Placement. Keep your feet flat on the ground or on a footrest, with your knees at a 90-degree angle. Arms should be relaxed at your sides, with elbows bent at 90 degrees.

Ergonomics While Driving

Long commutes or driving for extended periods can also lead to discomfort and pain. Adjusting your driving positions can significantly reduce this risk.

Seat Position. Adjust your seat so that your knees are level with your hips. If your seat allows, tilt it slightly backwards to support your spine's natural curve.

Steering Wheel Grip. Hold the steering wheel at a comfortable height, which should not force your shoulders to elevate or stretch forward. Your arms should be slightly bent.

Take Regular Breaks. If driving for long periods, take breaks to stretch and walk aound every hour or so to prevent stiffness and boost circulation.

Stretching and Movement

Incorporating stretching into your daily routine is essential for maintaining flexibility, improving mobility, and reducing chronic pain. Practice these simple daily stretching routines for pain management.

Neck and Shoulder Stretch
Gently tilt your head towards one shoulder until a stretch is felt on the opposite side of your neck. Hold for 15-30 seconds. Repeat on the other side. For shoulders, roll them back and down in a circular motion.

Upper Back Stretch
Extend your arms in front of you, clasp your hands together, and round your back, pushing your hands forward. Hold for 15-30 seconds to stretch your upper back.

Hamstring Stretch
Sitting on the edge of a chair, extend one leg out with your heel on the floor. Lean forward while keeping your back straight until a stretch is felt along the back of your though. Hold for 15-30 seconds and switch legs.

Spinal Twist
Sit on the floor wiith legs extended. Bend one knee and place the foot outside the opposite knee, using your elbow against the knee as leverage. Hold for 15-30 seconds and switch sides.

Movement Breaks to Reduce Stiffness and Pain To combat the stiffness and pain associated with prolonged sitting or standing, integrate short movement breaks into your day:

Walk Breaks. Every hour, take a five-minute walk. This could be around your office, home, or even in place.

Standing Stretch. Stand up, reach your hands overhead, and stretch upwards, then gently lean from side to side.

Chair Squats. From a sitting position, stand up without using your hands for support, then sit back down. Repeat 5-10 times to strengthen your legs and core, promoting better posture.

Adopting these stretching and movement practices can significantly contribute to managing chronic pain, enhancing your overall well-being. Remember, consistency is key. Start slowly and gradually increase the duration and frquency of your stretches and movements to build a healthier, more painfree body.

Mindful Posture Awareness

Incorporating mindfulness and breathing exercises into your daily routine can significantly impact your chronic pain management strategy, offering a non-pharmacological approach to reducing pain and enhancing overall well-being.

Mindfulness, the practice of being fully present and engaged in the moment, can be a powerful tool in managing chronic pain, especially when applied to posture awareness. By becoming more mindful of how we hold our bodies throughout the day, we can identify and correct poor posture habits that contribute to pain and discomfort.

Body Scan Technique. Start by performing a daily body scan. Close your eyes and mentally scan your body from head to toe, noting any areas of tension or discomfort. This practice helps in developing awareness of how different postures affect your body and pain levels.

Mindful Adjustment. When you notice areas of tension during your body scan, gently adjust your posture. Align your spine, relax your shoulders, and ensure that your feet are flat on the ground. Mindful adjustments can alleviate pain and prevent strain.

Breathing Exercises for Relaxation and Pain Relief Breathing execises not only promote relaxation but also play a role in pain management.

Diaphragmatic Breathing. Sit or lie down in a comfortable position. Place one hand on your chest and the other on your abdomen. Breathe in deeply through your nose, ensuring your abdomen rises more than your chest. Exhale slowly through your mouth. Repeat this process for several minutes, focusing on the sensation of breathing and the movement of your body.

4-7-8 Breathing Technique: Breathe in quietly through your nose for 4 seconds, hold your breath for 7 seconds, and exhale forcefully through your mouth, pursing your lips and making a "whoosh" sound, for 8 seconds. This technique can help reduce anxiety and pain perception.

Ergonomics at Home and Work

Ergonomics, the study of people's efficiency in their working environment, plays a crutial role in managing chronic pain, especially for those spending long hours at a desk or engaing in repetitive tasks at home. Applying ergonomic principles can signicantly reduce physical stress and prevent pain.

Workspace Ergonomics for Pain Prevention

Chair Selection and Adjustment. Choose a chair that supports the natural curve of your spine. Adjust the chair height so your feet can rest flat on the floor, and your knees are at or slightly lower than your hips.

Desk Setup. Ensure that your desk height allows your elbows to rest comfortably at a 90-degree angle. Position your monitor so the top of the screen is at or just below eye level, about an arm's lenght away, to avoid neck strain.

Keyboard and Mouse Placement. Keep your keyboard and mouse close to avoid over-reaching. Your wrists should be in a neutral position, not bent up or down.

Home Ergonomics to Support Well-being

Cooking and Cleaning. When performing tasks such as cooking or cleaning, maintain a neutral posture by bending at the knees instead of the waist. Use long-handled tools to avoid excessive bending or reaching.

Relaxing and Watching TV. Choose seating that supports your lower back. Avoid slouching or sitting in one position for too long. Use a footrest if your feet don't reach the floor.

Sleeping Posture. Invest in a mattress and pillows that support your spine. Try to sleep in a position that maintains the natural curve of your back, such as on your back with a pillow under your knees or on your side with a pillow between your knees.

By making these adjustments to your work and home environments, you can significantly reduce the risk of developing pain. Remember, the goal of ergonomics is to make your daily activities as confortable as possible, prevent pain before it starts.

Aromatherapy for Well-being

Aromatherapy uses essential oils derived from plants to promote health and wellness. Aromatherapy is a journey that engages the senses, emotions, and spirit. As you explore the world of essential oils, remember each scent carries its own story and potential for healing. Let your aromatic journey be guided by intuition, expert knowledge, and the natural rhythms of life, allowing these oils to be your companion.

Lavender is calming and reduces anxiety. Add a few drops to a warm bath, diffuse at home or office, or inhale directly when feeling overwhelmed.

Peppermint is energizing and improves focus. Inhale before a workout or diffuse in the morning when you need a boost.

Frankincense balances mood and relieves depression. Add to lotion and apply to wrists or behind ears when needing emotional centering.

Chamomile and bergamot aid sleep issues like insomnia. Spritz linen, spray on pillowcases, or consume in tea before bedtime.

Rosemary improves circulation and memory. Diffuse while studying to enhance concentration and retention.

Eucalyptus clears nasal congestion. Place a few drops on hands and inhale deeply. Also add to steamy showers.

Lemon uplifts mood and boosts immunity. Add a drop to your drinking water or smoothies.

When using, dilute oils properly and source 100% pure, therapeutic-grade varieties. Be cautious using while pregnant or for children. Aromatherapy is an easy, versatile way to incorporate the healing benefits of nature into daily wellness practices. Let uplifting scents nourish your body, mind and spirit!

Insights and Techniques for Aromatherapy

Aromatic Planting Guide: Encourage the cultivation of aromatic plants in home gardens or community spaces. This not only provides a direct source for essential oils but also enhances one's connection to the healing properties of nature.

Aromatherapy for Mindfulness and Meditation: Pair aromatherapy with mindfulness exercises and meditation practices. For example, using diffused lemon oil during a focus meditation or rose oil during a loving-kindness meditation.

Workplace Aromatherapy: Implement aromatherapy in the workplace to enhance focus and reduce stress. Oils such as rosemary can enhance concentration, while lavender can help manage work-related stress.

Aromatherapy in Daily Routines: Encourage the integration of aromatherapy into daily habits, such as adding a few drops of essential oil to morning showers or using a diffuser with a calming blend during evening wind-down routines.

Aromatherapy for Emotional Support: Explore the use of aromatherapy as part of emotional or psychological support, recognizing the ability of certain scents to evoke memories, emotions, and a sense of comfort or relief.

Reflexology for Holistic Healing

Reflexology applies pressure to specific points on the hand and feet that correspond to organs and systems. This activates nerve pathways to alleviate stress and restore homeostasis.

Practice Some Reflexology Techniques

For *anxiety relief*, massage the solar plexus reflex point on the ball of each foot using small circles with thumbs.

To *aid sleep*, use knuckles to apply firm pressure along the pituitary gland reflex on big toes.

For *headache relief*, knead the base of the nails on fingers and thumbs using gentle squeezes.

To *energize*, briskly rub the adrenal gland reflexes on the ball of each foot using knuckles.

To *relieve tension*, use thumb to massage the solar plexus reflex points on soles of feet.

For *digestion aid*, press circles on the stomach reflex below ball of feet.

To boost *immunity*, briskly rub the spleen reflex below the ball of the foot.

Zone Therapy Integration

Reflexology for Specific Conditions

AyuReflexology

Meridian-Based Reflexology

Aim for 5-10 minutes per foot or hand daily. Drink water afterwards to flush released toxins. Aoid reflexology with deep vein thrombosis, infections, or during pregnancy.

Restore harmony through this therapeutic practice passed down through generations. This ancient healing art for your hands and feet activates the body's innate healing. Rediscover the power of therapeutic touch with reflexology.

Acupressure for Balance

Acupressure applies targeted pressure to activate healing points along meridian lines. This clears blockage, restores flow, and brings the body into balance. As you delve into these acupressure practices, remember that each point pressed is a conversation with your body's healing intelligence.

Put in practice

Biofeedback-Informed Acupressure

Auriculotherapy Integration

Dynamic Acupressure Sequences

Acupressure for Emotional Release

Digital Acupressure Mapping

Collaborative Acupressure Workshops

Acupressure Toolkits

Intercultural Acupressure Exchange

Some Techniques to Try

For *headache relief*, press between thumb and index finger webbing using circular motions.

To *reduce anxiety*, firmly press on inner wrist crease three finger widths below palm.

For *improved sleep*, stimulate the ankle point on inner side three finger widths above heel.

To *alleviate nausea*, apply pressure to underside of forearm two thumbs above wrist crease.

For *nasal congestion*, pinch the fleshy web between thumb and index finger.

To *boost immunity*, use thumb to press on inside forearm three finger widths below crease.

For *mental focus*, squeeze wrists gently then briskly tap the back of hands.

ChiKobi Health's AcuZen acupressure bracelets provide continual stimulation through gentle pressure on key points. Pair with meditation, nutrition and rest.

This time-honored healing art brings balance to body and mind through the power of touch. Experience its benefits.

EMPOWERING WELL-BEING THROUGH FOOD

Welcome to a crucial segment of your journey towards holistic well-being – understanding the power and simplicity of food. In today's fast-paced world, the art of cooking and the joy of consuming whole, nutritious meals have been overshadowed by the convenience of processed foods. However, it's time to rekindle our relationship with what we eat and recognize the immense impact of food on our health.

The Simplified Kitchen: A Source of Nutritional Wealth

Frozen Vegetables: Your Nutrient-Rich Allies - Often overlooked, frozen vegetables are a treasure trove of vitamins and minerals. They are piked and frozen at their peak freshness, locking in essential nutrients. Quick to prepare and always available, they are perfect for stir-fries, soups, or as healthy sides.

Quick and Nutritious Meals Under 30 Minutes - Contrary to popular belief, preparing a nutritious meal doesn't have to be time-consuming. With a bit of planning and the right ingredients, you can whip up satisfying dishes that are both healthy and delicious. For instance, a quick vegetable stir-fry with quinoa or a hearty lentil soup can be both filling and nutrient-packed.

BREAKFAST

Veggie Omelet

Egg, spinach, mushrooms, cheese. Serve with fruit

Overnight Oats

Oats, chia seeds, milk, berries. Customize w/nut butter.

cinnamon

Tofu Scamble

Tofu scumbles sauteed with veggies and seasoning. Add avocado

LUNCH

Buddha Bowl

Base of quinoa or rice. Topped w/ roasted veggies, beans, nuts

Hummus Wrap

Whole grain wrap with hummus, roasted veggies, greens

DINNER

Veggie Curry

Curry simmered w/chickpeas, sweet potato & spinach. Over rice

Sheet Pan Fajitas

Chicken or beans, pepper, roasted onion. Wrap in tortillas

Reconnecting with Our Culinary Roots

Reviving the Lost Art of Cooking

For many of us, the generational transfer of cooking knowledge has been lost. However, it's never too late to learn. Cooking is not just about feeding ourselves; it's a form of self-care, an act of love, and a way to connect with our cultural heritage. It's about understanding what goes into our body and taking control of our health.

Empowerment Through the Kitchen

By reallocating a small amount of our time to prepare home-cooked meals, we gain more than just culinary skills. We empower ourselves to make healthier choices, understand our food better, and reclaim our health and well-being.

Healthy Homemade Meals

With a well-stocked kitchen, you can easily prepare nutritious meals at home. Try these delicious, wholesome recipes.

These simple yet nourishing homemade meals help you save money, reduce waste and control exactly what goes into your food.

Benefits of Home Cooking

Michael Pollan's Food Mantra - Renowned food journalist Michael Pollan offers a simple yet profound guide to eating: "Eat food. Not too much. Mostly plants." This approach encourages us to choose real foods over processed items, practice moderation in our portions, and focus on plant-based nutrition for better health and longevity.

Essential Kitchen Staples for Easy, Healthy Meals

Olive Oil: A versatile and healthy fat for cooking and dressings.

Onions and Garlic: Flavorful bases for most savory dishes.

Lemons: For a fresh zing in salads or to brighten up a dish.

Sugar and Salt: In moderation, to enhance the flavor of your meals.

Additional Ingredients: Whole grain pasta, canned salmon or tuna, vinegar, soy sauce, and fresh herbs like parsley, cilantro, and basil. These items are not only nutritious but also versatile, allowing you to create various dishes.

Sensible Substitutions for Long-Term Health

Addressing Unhealthy Cravings: Identify when you're most likely to choose unhealthy foods and find better alternatives. For instance, homemade popcorn instead of chips for a salty crunch, or homemade chicken nuggets instead of fast food.

Every Unhealthy Food Has a Healthy Counterpart: The idea is to swap, not to stop. This approach ensures that you're not depriving yourself of the foods you love but making them healthier and more nourishing.

Changing Our Fullness Mindset: Rather than eating to the point of being full, eat until you're no longer hungry. This subtle shift can significantly impact your long-term health and relationship with food.

Enriching Tips

Make cooking at home a weekly ritual

Involve family or roommates in cooking together

Start simple flexible recipes and fewer ingredients

Repurpose leftovers in creative ways

Stock your freezer with chopped vegetables

Batch cook sauces, dressings, & healthy croutons

Let a slow cooker be your helper

Make double batches and freeze half for later

Subscribe to a meal kit delivery service

Follow social media blogs focused on homecooking

Cooking and eating should be a joyful and nurturing experience. This section aims to equip you with the knowledge and tools to transform your eating habits, bringing you closer to achieving a balanced and healthy lifestyle. Remember, the journey to well-being begins in your kitchen!

Integrate Harmony in Daily Life

The journey to wellness is continuous and ever-evolving. Each day presents a new opportunity to integrate practices that resonate with your personal needs and lifestyle. Embrace the wisdom of holistic traditions and the latest research to craft a life that is not only healthy but also vibrant and fulfilling. Let each step taken be a conscious stride toward a more harmonious self and society.

Explore How to Effectively Incorporate Holistic Techniques into Your Lifestyle

Assess your needs and challenges first. Are you seeking more energy, calm, pain relief? Let this guide selection.

Identify optimal times to practice. Mornings energize, evenings induce calm. Schedule accordingly.

Start small. Even 5-10 minutes daily can make a meaningful impact over time.

Alternate techniques to prevent boredom. Try a new practice every few days.

Combine practices for enhanced benefits. Play calming music during acupressure or add oils to baths.

Create a sacred space. Candles, soft lighting and comforting environments invite practice.

Use reminders and prompts to build habits. Apps, wristbands or notes can reinforce rituals.

Reflect afterwards on impacts. Journal any insights and benefits from practices.

Make supplies visible and handy. Have bracelets, oils or cards on desk or nightstand.

Take classes for guidance. Yoga studios, community centers and online videos instruct.

Form or join a group. Shared experience provides motivation and accountability.

With experimentation, you'll discover what works best for your needs. Small steps towards inner wellness promise great rewards!

Put in practice

Value Assessment

Intentional Adjustment

Responsible Consumption

Community Investment

Financial Wellness Check-ins

Education and Growth

Clarify Values
What truly matters? Health? Knowledge? Legacy? Define your core values.

Categorize Expenses
Tally fixed and discretionary costs. Are all expenses essential?

Align with Values
Shift discretionary funds to support values. Donate or invest in personal growth.

Practice Mindful Spending
Pause before purchases. Do they serve your purpose and values?

Cultivate Gratitude
Appreciate what your budget enables, like security or giving.

Reflective Budgeting

Your budget is more than numbers on a spreadsheet; it is a reflection of your life's tapestry, woven with the threads of your values, choices, and aspirations. A valuebased budget empowers conscious spending furthering your vision - whether traveling the world or leaving a charitable impact. Money is simply potential. Direct it mindfully.

Your Health Story

By viewing our health stories through a lens of empowerment, we can move from passive characters to active authors, capable of crafting a narrative filled with growth, healing, and balance. Reframing our health stories with richness and compassion releases their ability to define or limit us. Our narratives become sources of meaning rather than suffering. This approach fosters a deeper connection with our inner selves and the external world, leading to a more fulfilled
and healthy life.

Consider your current health situation. What dominant story defines this experience? How might certain narratives limit or disempower you?

Put in practice

Re-examine the circumstances from different angles

What contextual factors surround your situation?

What resources, supports or solutions exist?
What small choices or changes could you make?

What meaning or growth could this experience provide?

What would a compassionate, wise advisor say about your story?

What "chapter" lies ahead if you were the author writing the tale?

Reframing our health stories with nuance, empathy and agency can open up new possibilities for healing. Share your narrative.

calm your mind

thoughts

Building Community

Each individual's contribution to the community is unique and valuable. As you weave your thread into the tapestry, remember that every interaction, every shared moment, and every collective triumph contributes to a stronger, more resilient community. Together, we can build a network of support that upholds values and extends the reach of holistic wellness in our lives.

Consider Creative Ways to Foster Community

Organize a story circle for people to share their health journeys in a judgment-free space. Provide encouragement and compassion.

Form support groups focused on specific health conditions, life stages, or cultural identities. Share resources and insights.

Use art, music, dance or theater to unite people across backgrounds. Express shared experiences through creative mediums.

Develop virtual communities via social media to exchange ideas, resources and encouragement.

Volunteer with local organizations supporting wellness initiatives and health access. Find purpose in service.

Partner with spiritual centers or community centers to offer classes, rituals, or gatherings exploring holistic wellbeing.

Advocate politically for health policies and funding supporting marginalized groups. Ensure care and access.

Establish workplace wellness programs promoting mental health, movement, and work-life balance. Prioritize meaning.

Foster intergenerational connections. Younger and elder community members have valuable teachings to exchange.

Help neighbors through meal trains, rides, childcare and other supports during health challenges.

Shared stories and struggles unite us. How will you cultivate community for wholeness? Whose light and wisdom could inspire your path?

Put in practice

Collaborative Wellness Challenges
Service Projects
Health Story Circles
Family and Friends Day
Community Gardens
Wellness Resource Sharing
Advocacy Groups
Virtual Connection Spaces

Global Wellness Practices

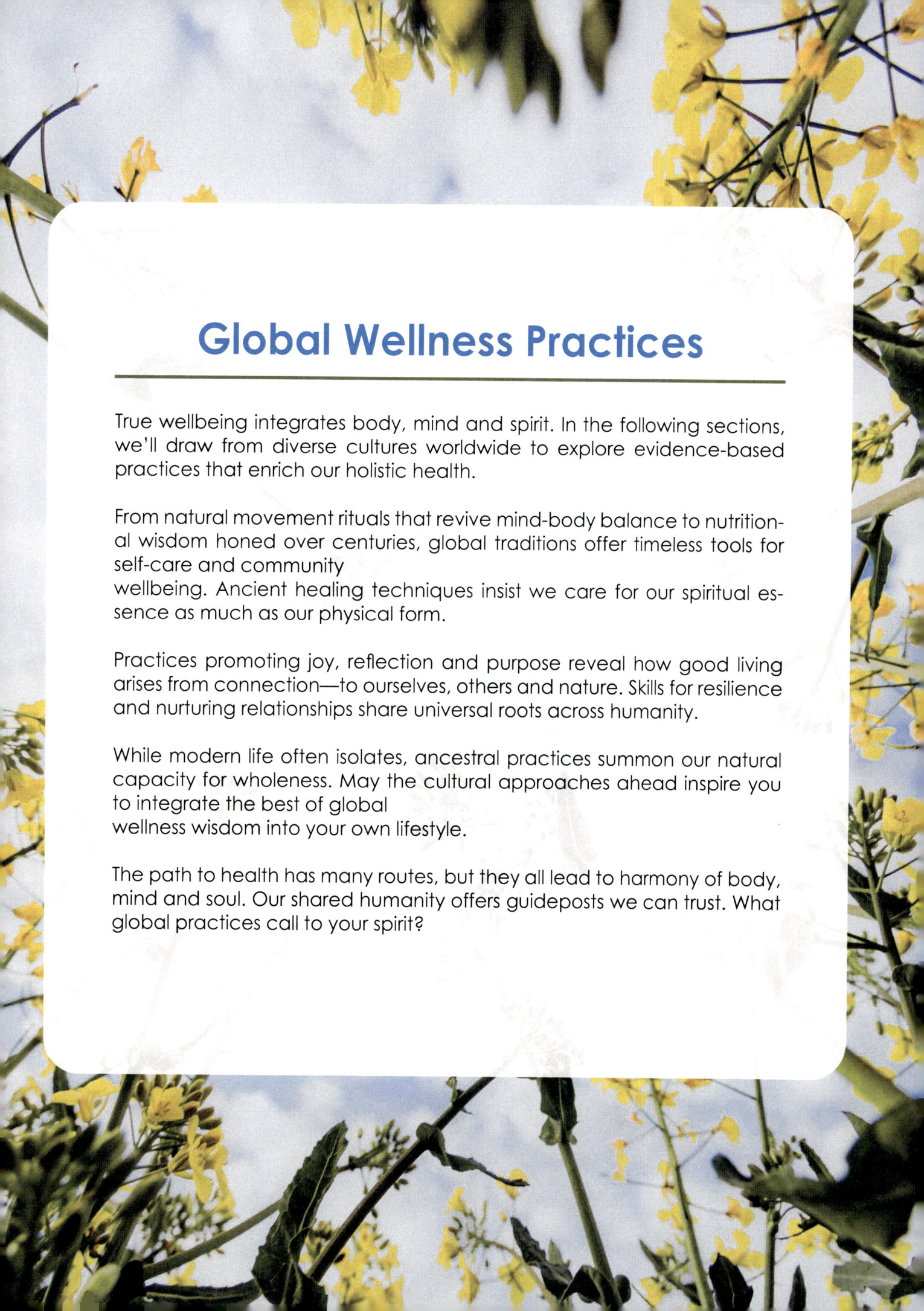

True wellbeing integrates body, mind and spirit. In the following sections, we'll draw from diverse cultures worldwide to explore evidence-based practices that enrich our holistic health.

From natural movement rituals that revive mind-body balance to nutritional wisdom honed over centuries, global traditions offer timeless tools for self-care and community
wellbeing. Ancient healing techniques insist we care for our spiritual essence as much as our physical form.

Practices promoting joy, reflection and purpose reveal how good living arises from connection—to ourselves, others and nature. Skills for resilience and nurturing relationships share universal roots across humanity.

While modern life often isolates, ancestral practices summon our natural capacity for wholeness. May the cultural approaches ahead inspire you to integrate the best of global
wellness wisdom into your own lifestyle.

The path to health has many routes, but they all lead to harmony of body, mind and soul. Our shared humanity offers guideposts we can trust. What global practices call to your spirit?

Natural Movement - Global Traditions

Welcome to Natural Movement, a section that introduces you to the world of holistic and traditional movement practices. Each of these practices is not just a physical exercise but a pathway to deeper well-being, integrating the mind, body, and spirit. Remember that each has its unique rhythm and flow. Respect your body's limits and immerse yourself in the experience, allowing these age-old traditions to rejuvenate your spirit.

Middle Eastern Dervish Whirling

Originating from the Sufi tradition, Dervish Whirling is a form of physically active meditation that's been practiced for centuries. This practice involves a repetitive spinning motion and is believed to bring about spiritual awakening, inner peace, and a deep connection with the divine. The swirling motion is symbolic of the planets orbiting the sun, representing a microcosm of the universal order.

Health Benefits: Enhances mental clarity, improves balance, increases focus, and provides a unique form of cardiovascular exercise.

Practice Tip: Begin with slow rotations and focus on your breathing. As you become more comfortable, gradually increase your speed.

Malaysian Bamboo Massage

This traditional massage technique uses bamboo canes of different lengths and diameters to roll and knead away aches and pains. It's deeply rooted in Malaysian culture and symbolizes strength, life, youth, prosperity, and peace.

Health Benefits: Promotes circulation, relieves stress, aids in lymphatic drainage, and provides deep relaxation.

Practice Tip: Seek a certified therapist to experience this unique massage technique, ensuring a safe and authentic experience.

Ubuntu African Drum Circles

'Ubuntu' translates to "I am because we are," reflecting the African philosophy of community and interconnectedness. African Drum Circles are more than rhythmic exercises; they are communal gatherings where people connect through the universal language of music.

Health Benefits: Drumming can reduce stress, increase feelings of well-being, boost the immune system, and enhance cognitive function.

Practice Tip: Participate in a drum circle with an open heart and mind. It's not just about keeping the rhythm but also about connecting with others.

Ancient Traditions...

Welcome to "Ancient Traditions," a section dedicated to exploring some of the world's most profound and time-honored wellness practices. Indigenous cultures worldwide developed holistic practices over millennia through deep connection with nature. Many still offer profound wisdom. These practices reflect the wisdom of various cultures and offer unique insights into holistic health.

Qi Gong

Qi Gong, a cornerstone of traditional Chinese medicine, combines movement, meditation, and regulated breathing to enhance life energy, or Qi. It's deeply spiritual yet immensely practical, helping practitioners achieve a state of balance and calm.

Health Benefits: Boosts mental and physical health by reducing stress, improving balance and flexibility, and enhancing immune function.

Practice Tip: Start with simple movements like "Cloud Hands" or "Gathering Heaven's Energy," focusing on breath control and fluidity of motion.

Peruvian Sound Healing

In Peru, sound is used as a healing modality, deeply rooted in the belief that the universe is composed of sound. Instruments like drums, flutes, and string instruments are used in ceremonies to promote healing and spiritual connection.

Health Benefits: Reduces stress and anxiety, promotes deeper sleep, and enhances emotional well-being.

Practice Tip: Listen to Peruvian music or participate in a sound healing session, allowing the vibrations to flow through and harmonize your body.

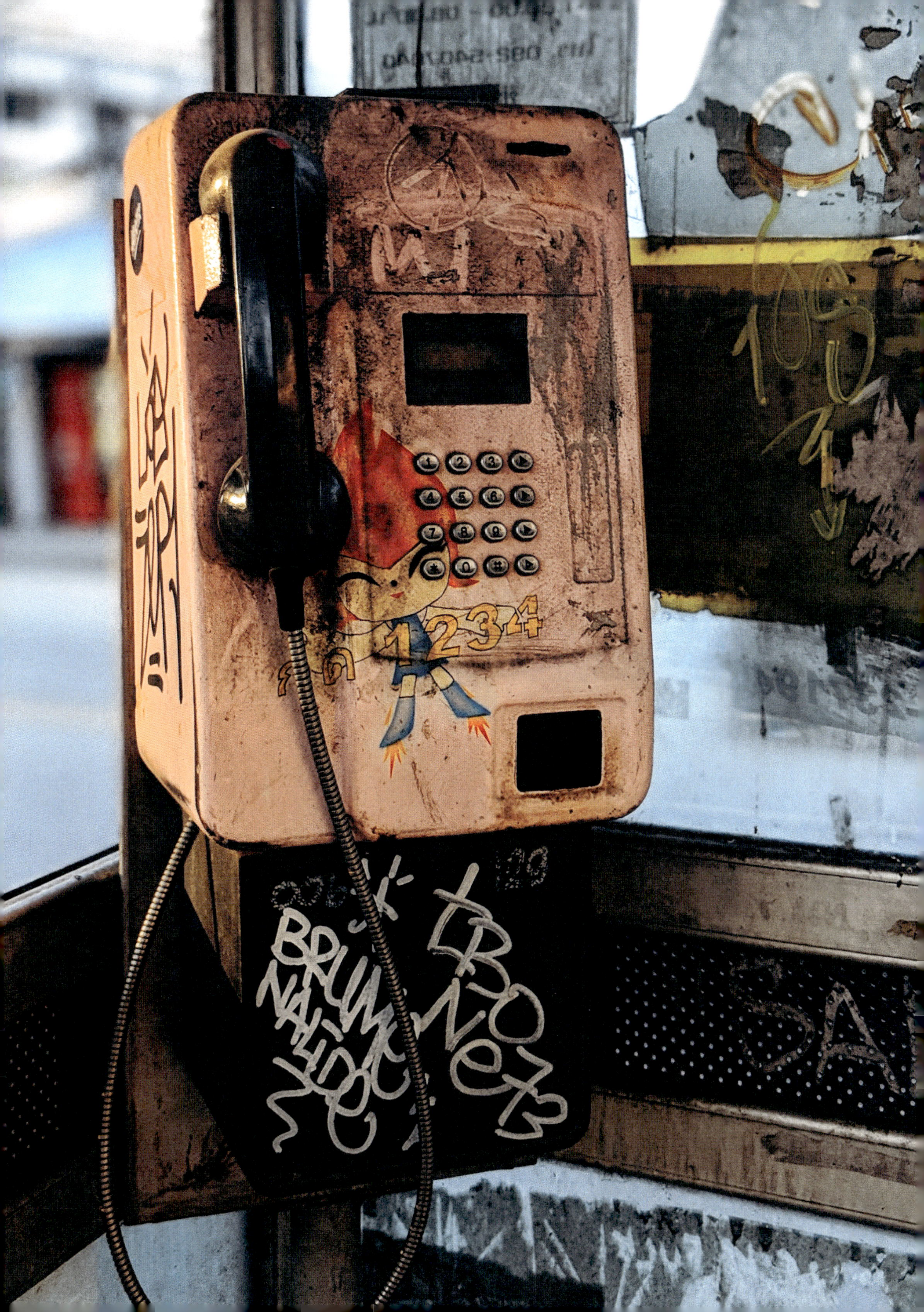
1234

...Wisdom from Across the World

It is encouraged to incorporate these ancient practices into modern life to deepen your understanding of global health traditions. By exploring these diverse approaches to wellness, you broaden your perspective and find new paths to personal health and fulfillment.

Ecuadorian Enduadorio

Enduadorio is a traditional Ecuadorian practice involving herbal baths and spiritual cleansing rituals. This practice is deeply intertwined with the Ecuadorian understanding of the connection between nature, health, and spirituality.

Health Benefits: Cleanses the body and spirit, promotes relaxation, and helps to reconnect with nature.

Practice Tip: Try creating a herbal bath at home using traditional herbs like rosemary, mint, and chamomile to experience a sense of purification and renewal.

Aboriginal Dreamtime

Aboriginal Australians have a profound spiritual tradition known as 'The Dreamtime.' It encompasses the creation stories and spiritual beliefs that explain the origins and culture of their world. Storytelling, art, and ceremonies are crucial aspects of this tradition.

Health Benefits: Strengthens community bonds, preserves cultural heritage, and offers deep insights into one's place in the universe.

Practice Tip: Engage with Aboriginal art and storytelling to understand this rich spiritual tradition better.

More Ancient Wellness Practices

Japanese Forest Bathing

Traditional Chinese Medicine

Ayurvedic Diet and Herbs

Cultural Healing: Embracing Restoration

In "Cultural Healing," we dive into the heart of diverse global practices that emphasize the importance of balance, rest, and connection in maintaining wellbeing. Diverse cultures have developed customs that promote community wellbeing. Here we'll explore traditions that enrich daily living.

Spanish Siesta Naps

In Spain, the traditional 'siesta' is more than just an afternoon nap; it's a cultural practice rooted in the understanding of the body's natural rhythm and the need for rest and rejuvenation.

Health Benefits: Enhances cognitive function, mood, and overall physical health. Reduces stress and boosts productivity.

Practice Tip: Incorporate a short, restful break into your daily routine, ideally after lunch, to disconnect and recharge, even if it's just for 15-20 minutes of quiet relaxation.

Korean Hanjeungmak

Hanjeungmak is an ancient Korean practice of visiting Hanjeungmak saunas, where high temperatures and steam are used to cleanse the body and relax the mind.

Health Benefits: Improves circulation, aids in detoxification, relieves muscle tension, and promotes skin health.

Practice Tip: Visit a Korean sauna or create a spa experience at home with a warm bath followed by a period of relaxation in a warm, quiet space.

Hygge: Art of Coziness

Originating from Denmark, 'Hygge' (pronounced "hoo-ga") is the art of creating warmth, connection, and contentment in everyday moments. It's about cherishing oneself, enjoying the company of loved ones, and feeling a sense of gratitude and coziness.

Health Benefits: Enhances mental wellbeing, fosters a sense of community and belonging, reduces anxiety and stress.

Practice Tip: Create a 'hygge' environment at home with soft lighting, comfortable blankets, and a warm drink. Dedicate time to simple pleasures like reading a book or enjoying a meal with family.

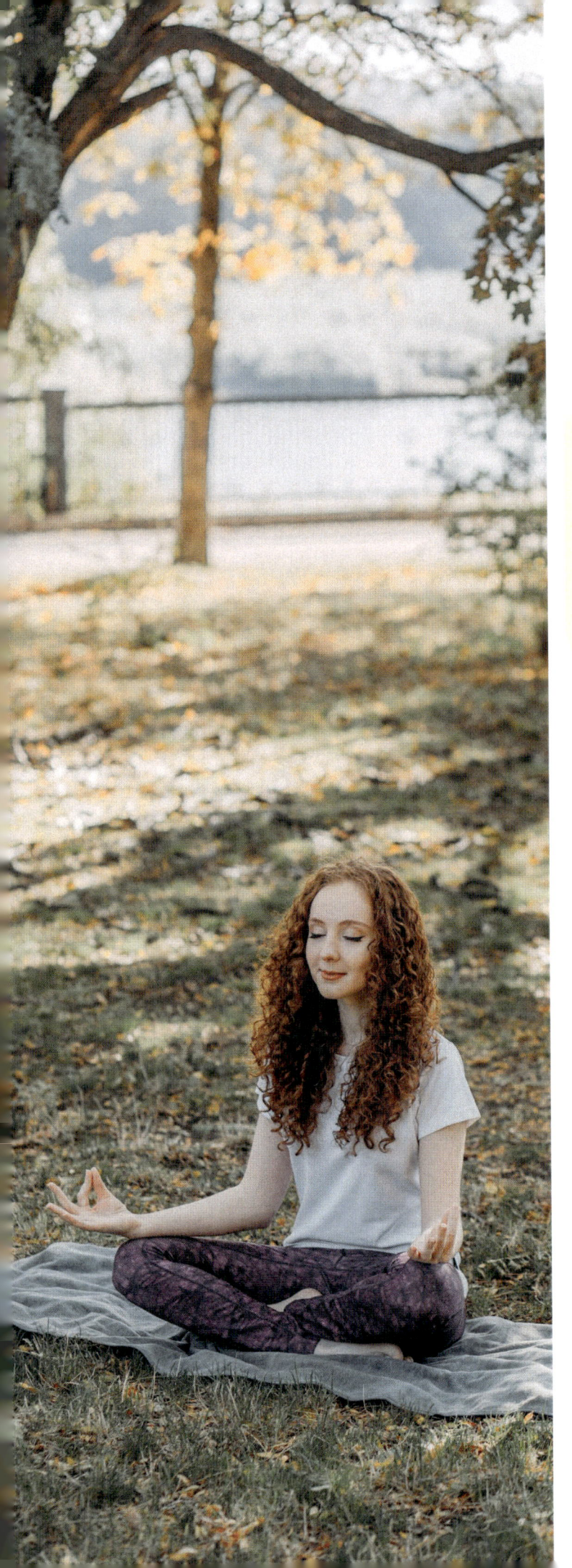

Isha Kriya Meditation

Isha Kriya, meaning "inner action", is a powerful meditation technique developed by Sadhguru, designed to enhance overall health and wellbeing. Accessible and simple, it's a perfect starting point for beginners to experience the profound benefits of meditation.

UNVEIL DEPTHS

Transcend the Physical and Mental

Harness the Power of Sound

Cultivate Inner Stillness

The Essence of Isha Kriya

This 15-minute guided meditation uses breath, thought, and awareness to increase your capacity to use your mind and body. It's an effective way to relax and rejuvenate, suitable for practice anywhere - at home, in the office, or outdoors.

Benefits for Body and Mind

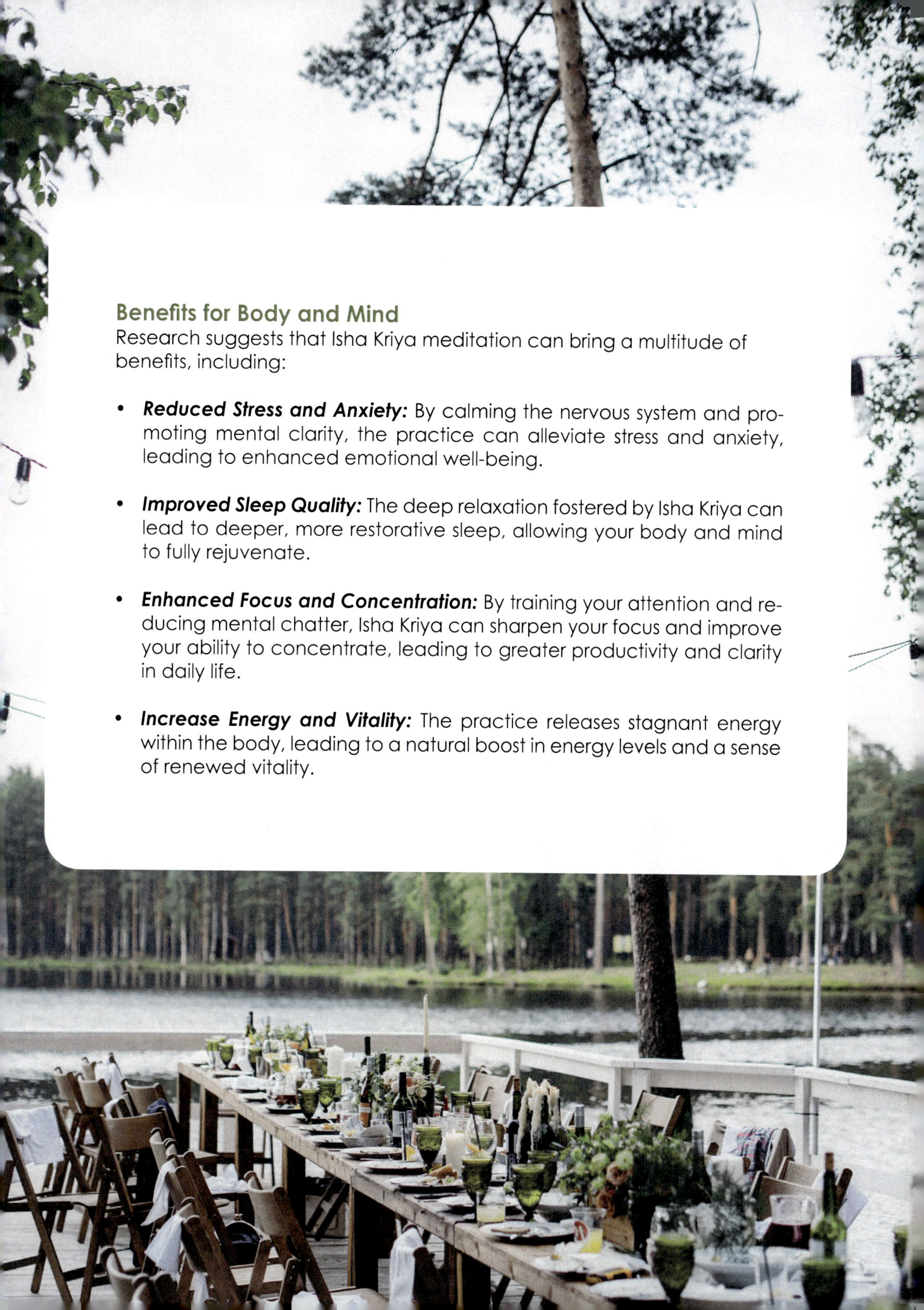

Research suggests that Isha Kriya meditation can bring a multitude of benefits, including:

- **Reduced Stress and Anxiety:** By calming the nervous system and promoting mental clarity, the practice can alleviate stress and anxiety, leading to enhanced emotional well-being.

- **Improved Sleep Quality:** The deep relaxation fostered by Isha Kriya can lead to deeper, more restorative sleep, allowing your body and mind to fully rejuvenate.

- **Enhanced Focus and Concentration:** By training your attention and reducing mental chatter, Isha Kriya can sharpen your focus and improve your ability to concentrate, leading to greater productivity and clarity in daily life.

- **Increase Energy and Vitality:** The practice releases stagnant energy within the body, leading to a natural boost in energy levels and a sense of renewed vitality.

Three Cycles Harmonizing Body and Mind

Through simple yet transformative techniques, this practice empowers you to experience a deeper sense of self. This ancient bija mantra (seed sound) resonates with the solar plexus, igniting inner energy and creating stability.

The Three Stages of Isha Kriya

First, find a confortable seated position: Sit with you back straight and eyes closed in a quient and distraction-free environment.

Stage 1: Awareness of Body and Mind

Duration: 7-11 minutes
Method:
1. Inhale deeply and slowly.
2. As you inhales, mentally repeat, " I am not the body." Exhale slowly.
3. As you exhale, mentally repeat, " I am not even the mind."
4. Ensure the duration of inhalation and exhalation matches the lenght of these thoughts.

This practice helps in detaching from physical and mental identities, fostering a deeper sense of inner peace.

Stage 2: Vocalizing the Sound "Aaa"

Duration: 7 times
Method:
1. With your mouth open wide, utter the sound "Aaa" seven times.
2. Focus on exhaling fully with each sound, feeling the vibration below the navel.

This sound vibration aids in energy realignment and creates a sense of balance within.

Stage 3: Upturned Focus and Relaxation

Duration: 5-6 minutes
Method:
1. Sit with a slightly upturned face and a mild focus between your eyebrows.
2. Stay relaxed and let the meditation deepen naturally.

Guideline for Effective Practice

FMind-Body Detachment: Ignore any physical or mental distractions. Let them exist without your engagement.

- **Continuity:** Avoid breaks during the practice to maintain the flow of energy.

- **Duration:** Practice for a minimum of 12 minutes each time.

- **Frequency:** Ideally, perform this Kriya twice a day for 48 days (a full mandala) or once daily for 90 days.

- **Universality:** This Kriya is suitable for everyone, irrespective of their meditation experience.

Finally, allow your mind and body to settle for a few moments before slowly opening your eyes. Carry the sense of peace and awareness throughout your day.

Isha Kriya is not a one-time fix, but an ongoing practice that unfolds its potent benefits over time.

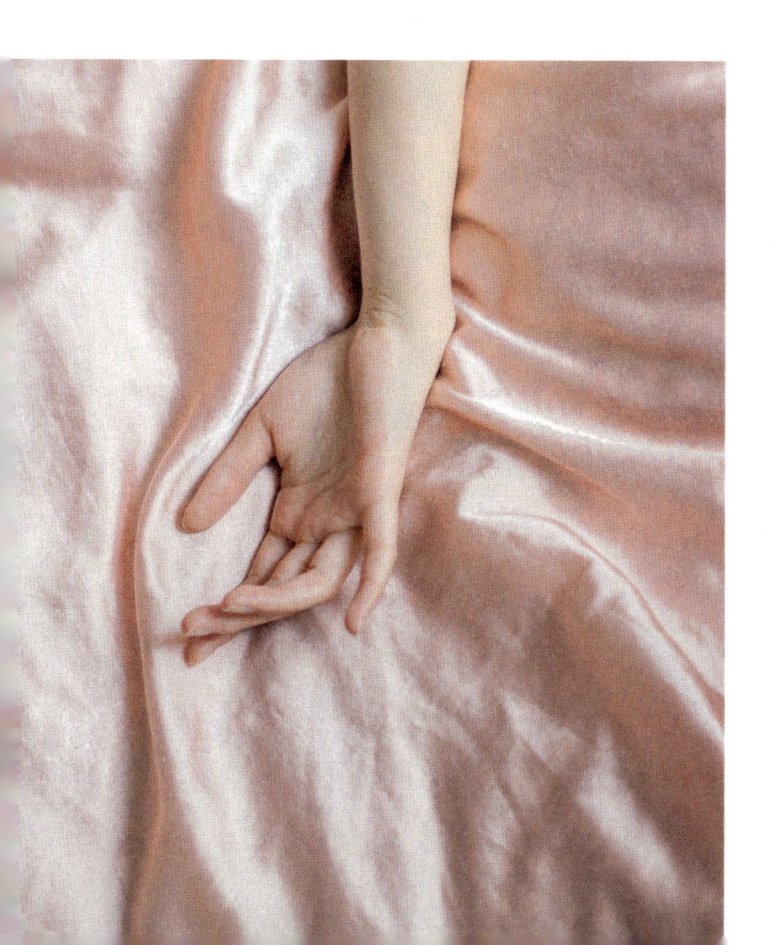

Your Journey Forward

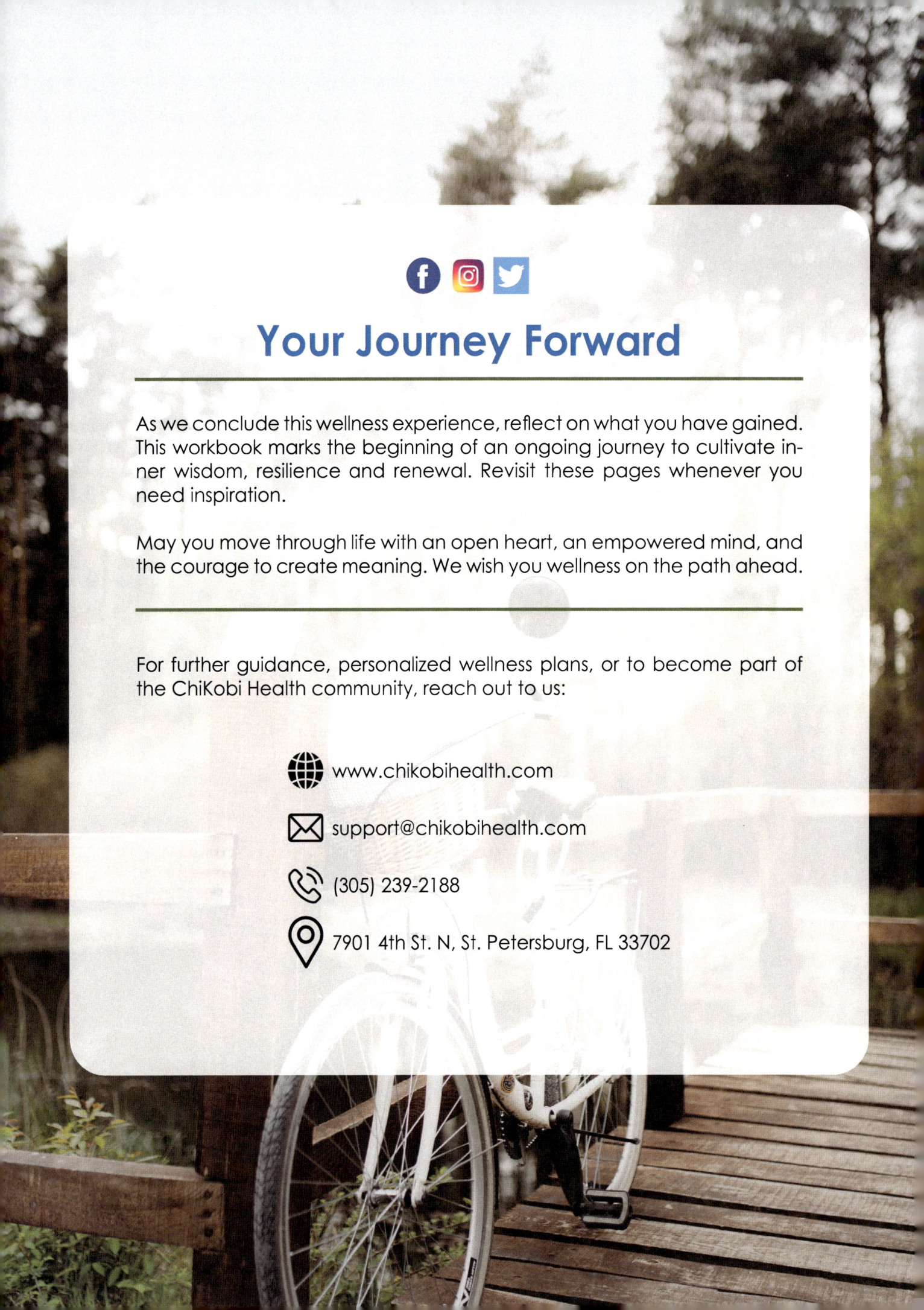

As we conclude this wellness experience, reflect on what you have gained. This workbook marks the beginning of an ongoing journey to cultivate inner wisdom, resilience and renewal. Revisit these pages whenever you need inspiration.

May you move through life with an open heart, an empowered mind, and the courage to create meaning. We wish you wellness on the path ahead.

For further guidance, personalized wellness plans, or to become part of the ChiKobi Health community, reach out to us:

🌐 www.chikobihealth.com

✉ support@chikobihealth.com

📞 (305) 239-2188

📍 7901 4th St. N, St. Petersburg, FL 33702